CONTENTS

FOREWORD

Well after they had retired, two Unitarian Ministers who have been friends for over fifty years started to clear years of accumulated books and papers. A chance phone call from Penny Johnson to Peter Hewis asked, "What should I do with all these prayers I have written?"

Peter thought they would be suitable for a small booklet and Penny then suggested that Peter should add some of his own.

By good fortune, Natasha Stanley, the Administrator of the Manchester District Association of Unitarian and Free Christian Churches, got to know what was proposed and offered to help, and took over all the work of the publication, and furthermore, obtained funding for the venture from the Manchester District Association. In the process, the booklet was extended to include some reflections from the pulpits of Penny and Peter to make it a larger and more worthwhile publication.

Both Peter and Penny have been involved in "Send a Child" since its beginnings sixty years ago, as Trustees and Leaders of holiday weeks. They decided that the proceeds of the sale of the publication would be given to that Charity, and since the cost of the printing and administration are to be borne by Manchester District Association, the Send a Child to Hucklow fund will receive every penny of what purchasers pay, which has been set at £5 a copy.

ABOUT THE AUTHORS

The Reverend Penny Johnson was educated at the Wolverhampton Technical High School then Manchester (now Harris Manchester) College, Oxford. She entered the Unitarian Ministry in 1976 and served ten congregations in the West Midlands for five years before moving to Styal, Hale, and Dean Row Chapels in Cheshire until her retirement in 1998. As a teenager she helped to pioneer a Sunday School at her home church, Wolverhampton, and was a Lay Preacher for ten years in the Midland Union Churches.

Her Secretarial experience was invaluable to ministry, particularly in organising her time and work schedules, and for fourteen years she was the General Secretary of the Manchester District Association of Unitarian and Free Christian Churches.

Music has played a large part in her life. As a violinist, she has been a member of a number of local orchestras and the National Schools Orchestra, and as a horn player, a member of Poynton Royal British Legion Concert Band as well as its Chaplain. She is very involved with the Unitarian Music Society. Penny is a member of the Unitarian Women's League and has been both District and National Presidents.

In 1988 she married Ken Johnson at Dean Row Chapel Wilmslow and acquired three adult stepchildren, Carol, Sandra, and Robert.

The Reverend Peter Hewis trained at the Unitarian College in Manchester and Manchester University. He had Ministries in Bethnal Green, Hinckley and then became Chaplain, Bursar and Tutor in Ministerial Training at Harris Manchester College in Oxford.

Music also plays a large part in his life. From 1958-61 he played cornet then French Horn with the Band of the 2nd Bn. Parachute

Regiment and in retirement plays Tenor Horn with Yarnton Band in Oxfordshire.

Peter and his wife Heddwen have two children, Bethan is a fashion designer who also runs the Brinsley Animal Rescue Centre and Griffith is a sound engineer specialising in classical music.

REFLECTIONS

AND IT WILL NEVER BECOME JUST WHAT WE PLANNED

Have you ever had a phrase going through your mind for days, and you think, "where have I heard that before?" The words, "And it will never become just what we planned" haunted me for about a week. I went through readings and prayers trying to locate them, but in vain, and quite suddenly I knew: "Seasons of the Soul" by American Unitarian Universalist Minister, Robert Terry Weston. I am a great list maker, I write down everything I want to achieve in a day, but then the day is so often turned upside down by a telephone call or something more pressing than anything on the list. Does that happen to you? An hour, a day, a week, a month, a year, life itself cannot be trapped, pinned down, and made to conform to our best endeavours. I like Robert Terry Weston's notion that a year can begin any time we like, such as today: and whatever lies ahead of us – all the raw stuff of human experience, waiting for us to fashion as we will, will never become just what we planned.

We can apply this dictum to interruptions, or events, or circumstances.

I like to think that I am in control of my life, and that I shape it: do you? I like to tick off tasks accomplished, so unexpected interruptions will delay this. Some people thrive on interruptions: the more the better because they postpone the inevitable "getting down to the task in hand" and from my experience people of this kind are very relaxed about life; they seem to be unhurried, with time for everyone, you never feel that you are interrupting their busy schedule because they don't seem to have any grasp of time. It must be wonderful to be so easy going. The words, "and it will never become just what we planned" have no place in their scheme of things because there doesn't seem to be a plan. Eventually whatever they have to accomplish will get done, but not yet. Even in my retirement I cannot quite achieve this sense of ease.

One interruption which was not so welcome when it happened, but brought a considerable bonus, was when I was doing my finals in the Diploma in Social Studies in Oxford, and there was a knock at my door: it was the Chairman of the College Council, who wanted to borrow a towel. Panic set in. Last minute revision had to take a back seat while he regaled me with stories, but, very importantly, he told me of his experiences of Community Associations in Scotland, and believe it or not, I was able to use the information in one of my essays on the Social Administration paper that very afternoon in 1975. The thought, "when is he going?" turned into, "thank goodness he came." With hindsight, it was a most welcome interruption, for which I was immensely grateful.

It might seem to us that just as we are forgeing ahead with some project or plan, into our organised world come crises, family illness, or our own illness or needs of others, which must, of necessity, take priority over everything else. We have to put our own plans on hold. Sometimes we lurch from crisis to crisis and don't know which way to turn. So much for us controlling our own lives! Our lives are now being determined by other people and we wonder just how much time and energy we ought to devote to these other people (however close they happen to be to us). Every situation is going to be different. But perhaps you will recognise the general scenario. I remember a time when my husband Ken was ill in bed one Sunday morning, the doctor was expected, I was due to conduct morning services, my mother, in no uncertain terms told me that my place was with Ken. Ken was telling me that there was nothing I could do by staying, the doctor arrived and said, "Go." Life takes us in several directions at once. There are dilemmas. But by contrast I was able to ask a colleague to conduct an afternoon service for me when my mother was taken to hospital and needed me there. Such decisions have to be made quickly and responsibly...it will never be just what we planned.

Sometimes we are almost guided to say "no, I'm sorry" feeling the need to pace ourselves, and say, we are not puppets on strings to be pulled by other people, we have our personal limits of energy and time. Those words by the theologian of the nineteenth century, the Rev. Dr. James Martineau, are at times particularly poignant: "Since we know not what a day may bring forth, but only that the hour for serving thee is always present, may we wake to the instant claims of thy holy will, not waiting for tomorrow but yielding today." And I take it that those instant claims are bound up with our responsibilities to those around us who need us.

Do we have any plan in mind when we visit a friend who is ill? There are people who tell me that they cannot go to see their friends who very ill because they will not know what to say, and my response has been, "go, and be there, listen and respond. Don't be afraid of not knowing what to say. The important thing is to go".

For myself, I was very conscious of "weakness" when I visited one particular person. I entered the hospital room, and felt tears pricking the backs of my eyes and fought to recover. How could I face her? All my training said, "you don't do that, you have to be strong. Tears are the last thing she needs. A voice said, "Penny, come here." She embraced me and said, "thank you for your tears. They tell me you care." How gracious. I had gone to help her, and what happened was that she helped me and in that moment for both of us there was a deeper experience beyond strength or failure. It was certainly not what was planned. I couldn't have planned that if I had tried.

There are major crises to which we have to give our attention. When my mother went into hospital for the last time there was a suggestion by the consultant that she should have an exploratory operation. She was 98. I asked, "Wouldn't it be kinder to let her slip away?" Not a question he wanted to answer, and all his body language indicated this, but in the event, he decided not to operate, largely because the anaesthetist was unhappy, and we were told to look for a nursing home for her. We had promised her that our home would always be hers, so when she asked when she could come home, which was really all she wanted to do, I told her as gently as I could that we would be unable to look after her, even though we had promised to do so, but the care she needed was not something we could give. For a long time, I regretted this, because she died a few days later. I had let her down. Hindsight is a wonderful thing, but she was a woman who always wanted to know the truth, and I couldn't lead her to believe that she would come home when she wouldn't. I shared this with a Consultant in Palliative Care at Oxford University, who worked in the Oxford Hospitals. She told me something which was immensely helpful, which I want to pass on to you, in the hope that it will help any of you in a similar position: she said, "You were right to tell her. She needed to know." I told her I felt that my mother had decided to die when she knew she couldn't return home, and that when she died, regrettably, I was not there. She said that although no study had been carried out, in her experience people often did one of two things, either they waited until the whole family was at the bedside, or they waited until everyone had gone, but they took charge, they took control of their own deaths. I found that illuminating, fascinating and very comforting to know. In my wildest dreams the outcome was so different from what I had expected, and another powerful example of the "and it will never become just what we planned."

In all these cases of course, we have to be "flexible" - re-arrange our timetables to accommodate the unexpected, put other people first, and shelve what we had planned for ourselves. The best made plans go wrong, and you will undoubtedly have instances in your lives when your world was turned upside down by one event, one unexpected happening, trivial or large, and all you can do is what seems right at the time. Living with "if only" or "what might have been" is not an option.

Sometimes we who believe that we control and shape our lives and make things happen have to admit that some things are beyond our control: other people's desires and dreams, wishes and decisions impinge upon our own, and we cannot be responsible for everyone, in fact we shouldn't even try. It might even be arrogant to believe it. Sometimes we might make a passing nod to the idea that there is such a thing in this universe as "destiny" what happens to us and to those closest to us was "in our stars" all along, out of our hands altogether – not always an attractive idea to Unitarians who like to believe in the ability to think and decide for ourselves on how our lives will develop, but more and more perhaps we look at circumstances and say, "it was meant to be." Decisions and tasks, drudgery, achievement and defeat, joy, and grief, all the raw stuff of human experience, waiting for us to fashion as we will. **And it will almost never become just what we planned. Amen**

Penny Johnson

SERVE THE LORD WITH GLADNESS

A sermon first preached during the General Assembly Meetings of Unitarian and Free Christian Churches in 2001 at Chester Cathedral

When I was a child there were no Sunday outings. Sundays were set aside for church. My father was the chairman of our church at Wolverhampton, and he felt duty bound to be there. I think it is true to say that our lives revolved round the church. I make no criticism: merely state the facts. I suspect that it will also be true for many of you here this evening. Looking back, I see that this is when my own commitment to the church, both locally and nationally began.

Everyone here tonight knows beyond any shadow of doubt that we are **all** vital to the life of our churches. Each of us is important, and each of us valuable and if we can serve with gladness, we uplift all those around us who share the task. We serve by being part of a church which serves the whole person and the whole community, from which will come the hopes and ideals of a better world.

If we think for a moment of what is going on in our own church or churches, all the people involved - the officers, committees, choir perhaps, children's group, minister, or lay leader, those who take on responsibilities for social activities; then widen the vision to include all the other churches, both here and in other parts of the world, all the District Associations, and Committees of the General Assembly and add to these all those who write articles for our journals, the General Assembly President and everyone at our Headquarters; and our Colleges; we shall get some idea of the level of Service already offered. It is phenomenal. Without it we should DIE....and I think it is time to say publicly. THANK YOU...THANK YOU FOR ALL YOU DO ALREADY, AND ALL THAT YOU WILL CONTINUE TO DO BECAUSE YOU VALUE YOUR CHURCH and more, because you recognise that by serving your church with gladness, you are also furthering the purpose of God, whatever you conceive God to be. I have taken the words of the Psalm One Hundred: "Serve the Lord with Gladness"...you may wish to express it differently: but however, it is expressed, JOY should be at the heart of it.

Think for a moment of the alternative: where there is no joy, only a sense of despondency and gloom. Despair feeds upon itself. If the congregation has dwindled dramatically, a choice may have to be made as to whether to close, limp along, or find some way of injecting freshness into an otherwise dire situation: questions are asked: "has everything been done that can be done?" "has all the available help been obtained? "That is not idle speculation. It is very real and very sad to those who have given a lifetime's service to their churches. We know that desperate situations CAN be turned round, and with a little ingenuity, the Chapel can prosper once more. Persevering grudgingly, despairingly, joylessly will serve little purpose, and merely postpone a decision to close, for moribund churches can never adequately cater for the spiritual needs of a congregation. Spiritual needs are many and various. Some of them are obvious, such as time for prayer and reflection, a time to listen and to share concerns; a time to make a joyful noise unto the Lord and come before his presence with singing - some are less obvious. I feel we should never underestimate the power or the blessing of humour and laughter. Years ago laughter in church would have been unthinkable, but nowadays it seems a natural part of a church service, it is one of the elements of a service which newcomers remark upon, and which attracts them, and even keeps them with us. They tell their friends, "We really enjoy the services." Laughter is as natural as breathing. It should not be contrived but adds to a happy joyful atmosphere. People at Dean Row Chapel still remember the day that my cat "Pinocchio" came to church. The rain was torrential and Pinocchio (or Noki as he was more generally known) made his way round the outside of the chapel building pressing his little face against each window in an effort to find me. He could hear me, but he could not see me. He howled and howled, but we didn't let him in. On reflection perhaps we should have done. The service survived because of the pure tolerance of the congregation and by missing out the silent prayer. Eventually I said, "If you have noticed a cat outside, it's mine. He followed me to the chapel this morning," where upon the Chapel secretary, Arnold Kay, sitting in the back pew said. "He should be up there in the choir." (The choir are above us in the organ gallery). On a different occasion the chapel choir was the target of a remark from a small boy, who said quite loudly, "Look Mom, there are the muppets."

People enjoy worshipping in a relaxed and happy atmosphere. They enjoy the homely feel of eating simnel cake on Mothering Sunday, and when a wooden offertory box falls to bits as it is being carried forward during the service, and the entire offertory spills out on the floor, they enjoy the moment. Effectively handling embarrassment is also, therefore, a service we render to each other, so that we can somehow incorporate it into an otherwise dignified service with ease.

Where possible, everyone who is willing to make a contribution to church life should be encouraged to do so and those who look as though they might, if approached, find their own niche should be given the opportunity. I am a great believer in getting everybody involved so that they feel part of the church family. We are not a closed club: we are a team, sharing the responsibility of making our church as good, as open, as excellent as it can be. WE ARE OUR OWN BEST ADVERTISEMENT AND NO POSTERS, WAYSIDE PULPITS, OR OTHER FORMS OF ADVERTISEMENT CAN POSSIBLY REPLACE THE IMPACT THAT THE CHURCH ITSELF MAKES UPON A NEWCOMER. Every one of us is important to that total impact, to the tone of the place, to that welcoming atmosphere. We are all part of the quality of service offered where all are valued.

And how can we all be valued when the few at the top do everything? When the few at the top have always done everything and have never bothered to look beyond "the way it has always been done." "Enabling" is a completely new world to them, sadly, and yet enabling others is one of the most vital aspects of service we can offer. We should find out immediately what particular strengths and gifts they possess and draft them in with gusto. Just imagine where the Christian church would have been if Jesus had completed his ministry and left nothing to be accomplished by those who followed: they took up the challenge of continuing his ministry, and we take up a further challenge of continuing it today and will pass on that responsibility to those who come after us. We can be sure that there will be much still to do. Every new generation brings its own vision and today we rejoice that the climate is ripe for different religious faiths and cultures to work together, grow in understanding, and build a better and more acceptable world for us all.

I wonder where I might have been today if all who have helped me on my way had not enabled me to be a minister. If they had not helped me to achieve something of my potential; if they had not seen at least a little spark of light and fanned it into a flame. Where would you be if people around you had not enabled you to develop yours? I have often quoted the words of William Shakespeare concerning Julius Caesar, who was so delighted to have reached his zenith that he forgot all those people who had paved the way for him: who had helped him up to the top of the ladder. "He then unto the ladder turned his back, scorning the base degrees by which he did ascend." I believe it is tremendously important to acknowledge, with every ounce of gratitude, the inspiration and aspiration we have been fortunate enough to receive from those who have toiled with great patience and love to enable us to have become what we are. And the best way of showing appreciation, surely, is to make our experience available to others who might welcome it. But I am equally conscious that what each of us as an individual human being is doing is part of a much larger and varied picture, the greater part of which is as yet unknown, and still to be shaped by future generations.

Nor do I believe that those who offer their experience to others who follow do so with any hope of reward, at least, not if it is to be of real and lasting service. It is a matter of responsibility: we are all in this together, young, and old alike, doing what we can to ensure that we offer the best of ourselves.

But although we may not have "reward" in mind, it is a pleasure to see someone's sterling contribution being properly and appropriately acknowledged. I wonder how many silver salvers are sitting proudly on table tops up and down the country, or cards signed by the entire congregation to mark a special occasion, scrap books of important congregational events, chalice earrings and necklaces given as tokens of appreciation to worthy recipients, or special testimonials and illuminated addresses hanging in prominent positions in the home which say, "thank you for a lifetime of service" and which are rightly treasured. All these speak volumes: service offered with joy and gladness is not taken for granted, but valued, and those who give the service, so gladly, cherished.

As one of the older ministers (now technically retired) but with some energy and experience to offer, I love to listen to the younger ministers. I love their fresh approach. I am also conscious of the vast and valuable service given to the Denomination by our Lay Leaders and Lay Preachers, all of whom are confronted week by week and year by year with the task of leading good worship, enlivening our churches and providing a spiritual home for congregants.

I am also thankful for fresh opportunities to continue to serve our churches, and the people in them. Retirement doesn't mean stopping work but changing direction. I have always held the view that each of us is a minister, serving one another as our gifts and talents dictate. Ministry is very much a congregational affair. If we had to rely on our one trained congregational leader to attend to every detail of ministry, we might wonder whether the church would survive, but in truth there is a larger ministry by members themselves in all sorts of appropriate ways, sometimes spiritual and sometimes practical. We heard the wise words of Jesus Ben Sirach, "Each is skilful in his own craft." That is **everyone. We need the academically bright, but we also need those with every possible skill "to maintain the fabric of the world." It is merely a question of where we can put our best efforts. EVERYONE IS IMPORTANT. Jesus himself, for instance, as a carpenter, would have combined intellect with practical wisdom.**

At best we are all involved in offering "Service" with joy and gladness. Our churches depend upon <u>every one</u> of us to make a difference, and if anyone feels too small or too insignificant to make a difference, consider this saying: "Anyone who thinks they are too small to make a difference has not been in bed with a mosquito."

If we **make a difference** by our devotion and commitment, we **ourselves gain from the service we offer.**

It is a human need to be used for the larger good. Have you noticed how older members of our congregations so often lament the fact that they cannot contribute in the way they used to and they feel useless. Congregations can often respond positively and find such people an appropriate way of making a valid contribution. As a little illustration, my mother- in -law, who lives in a residential home, helps children from a local school to learn to read: they are brought to her, with the result that they are given help, and she does something positive. She is ninety-eight. She does something valuable for the community.

Few of us want to give up serving and serving gladly. George Bernard Shaw said: "This is the true joy of life; the being used for a purpose recognised by yourself as a mighty one. I am of the opinion that my life belongs to the whole community, and as long as I live, it is a privilege to do for it whatever I can. I want to be thoroughly used up when I die, for the harder I work, the more I live. I rejoice in life for its own sake. Life is no brief candle to me. It is a sort of splendid torch which I have got hold of for a brief moment, and I want to make it burn as brightly as possible before handing it on to future generations. life is no "brief candle" to me. It is a "splendid torch". We might add: "It is a Liberal light which shines in the neighbourhood, in the world, all the time." Or, for those of us who go back a little further in time, "Jesus bids us shine like a pure clear light, like a little candle, burning in the night. In this world of darkness, so we must shine, you in your small corner, and I in mine." It is the same thought differently expressed in different terms. And how better to "keep our chalice alight" than to offer the kind of service which engages us in serving one another joyfully and selflessly? In our reading from the writings of Freya Stark, we heard the words: "Service endows people with their chance of the greatest of worldly luxuries, since it makes of their labour a thing that can be given. It is to service, which is the Cinderella among human qualities, that the gift of organisations belongs. She achieves and is not feared. And perhaps we are all waiting for the moment when arrogance and self-aggrandisement, those domineering sisters, are put in their proper place by the kitchen fire, and the princes of this world find the little glass slipper of their neglected love. "

It is this spirit of service which here we celebrate today, where giving and receiving are part of a single action.

I am certain that we shall all have our own illustrations of the spirit of service. Twenty- five years ago as a very new minister in the West Midlands, I took the Reverend Dudley Richards to a ministers' meeting in Kidderminster, (an ecumenical group of ministers). He was then the Vice Principal of Manchester College, Oxford, and had been taking services in the West Midland Churches. The secretary introduced him as the Reverend Dudley Richards, who was assisting Penny Laws. I mentioned this to him later, a little embarrassed that he had been relegated to be my assistant, and he replied, "But that is exactly what I am, and pleased to be so."

My husband Ken and I saw something of this same spirit of service at a hotel in Winchester. Our cases were immediately conveyed to our rooms by a male member of staff. We later saw the same person serving in the dining room, and a few nights later in the very busy coffee shop belonging to the hotel, trying to work under almost impossible conditions. "Never mind" said Ken, "One day you will be the Head Waiter." He smiled, and replied, "**I am the Head Waiter.**"

It was in this spirit that Jesus responded to the question: "who is the greatest of all?" and his reply rather disarmed his disciples. He told them that greatness could not be measured in terms of power or authority, but in the ability to put oneself last. It was not the answer they expected, and they were challenged to address the idea of service where the greater good is everything and self-importance is deplored. It is in this light that we are challenged to serve one another and God.

I am particularly fond of a saying of an Indian philosopher, Vivekanda, who said, "Be grateful to those you help. Think of them as God. Is it not a privilege to serve God by helping your fellows?"

And so, friends, let us never underestimate our own efforts. Believe that our efforts make a difference: remember the saying: "anyone who thinks they are too small to make a difference has not been in bed with a mosquito." Let us never undervalue the service we give either to our churches or to our community or to the world. TO SERVE THE LORD WITH GLADNESS, (or if we would prefer, TO SERVE THE HIGHEST WE KNOW, JOYFULLY) IS A WONDERFUL PRIVILEGE. Amen

Penny Johnson

VISIT TO ROCHDALE
ART GALLERY

Some time ago, my husband Ken and I visited Rochdale Art Gallery and I was particularly taken by two pictures, both by women artists. The first was by Henrietta Ward, wife of the distinguished artist Edward Matthew Ward. Her **maiden** name was Ward, and she came from a family of painters. She fell in love with Edward when she was eleven and he was twenty-seven, and they married secretly and had eight children.

The painting was called, "The Princes in the Tower." What struck me forcibly about it was that all the furniture and objects in the painting were far better executed than the faces of the princes. While they did not even look like real people, a small highly polished table, a copper bowl, a wonderful tablecloth, with excellent folds, a dish with a perfect ellipse, a spoon with foreshortened handle were all a delight. The table was laden with delicious, sumptuous food, a roast chicken, a loaf of crusty bread, a jug of wine, all of which you felt you could pick up and hold, and in the case of the food, eat! Painting any of these would have presented challenges to the artist to make them so realistic. But the two princes in the tower were not so well executed. They were huge compared with everything else. The quality of the central figures paled into insignificance beside the incidentals. It might have been better to have left them out of the picture altogether and give the picture another title. There may be others who would not agree, but art is subjective.

Nearby was a picture by Jessica Halliday, who lived from 1858-1940. This featured a little girl seated at a table looking out of the window. The child, the table and chair dominated the picture. It was to all intents a picture of the furniture in the room, **but** the title of the painting was, surprisingly, "The Robin." I asked Ken, "Can **you** see the Robin?" We looked more closely, we struggled to see it, and then, finally, we saw it: **this tiny bird on the windowsill**. It really required a magnifying glass to see it. The Robin was the tiniest thing in the picture. The Artist had considered that the tiniest bit of the picture deserved to be the most important.

I was struck by the incidentals in the first picture being so lifelike while the central figures were flat and "wooden" and the title of the second picture being the very thing you struggled to see, the Robin.

What message are we supposed to find in these works of art?

Perhaps that the smallest detail could be the most important thing there.

That we are to concentrate on the small and insignificant amid the obvious. **Nothing** is too small to be important, and that includes each one of us. At best we are all important. Our churches, for instance, depend upon every one of us to make a difference.

I have a book at home "To those who see" by a distinguished American artist and writer, Gwen Frostic. It has hand-made paper and an actual leaf pressed between the paper leaves of the book, and right at the end a pressed butterfly. It begins, "To those who see. The wildness calls, and in the snow are tracks that lead us on. The winds blow freshness to our lives and stars seem close enough to touch." It ends with the words, "Caterpillar, cocoon, butterfly, can not one believe in miracles?" and we can add that the use of all our senses is so important to our understanding.

I attend an Art Class in Bollington, near Macclesfield on Tuesday mornings and know how vital it is to see, really see, what we are copying: to spend a period (even half an hour or more) just getting to know the object completely and intimately, before putting pencil to paper to absorb its uniqueness, its characteristics, and then communicate what we see to paper. It is the ability to **see** it which is the most important thing.

We can look and look and fail to really see what is there, for instance, the object's height and depth and relationship with other objects in the picture in terms of texture, light and dark and distance. Our senses are so vital, as are the way we look and the way we see. For example, when someone is sharing a problem with us it is important not only to hear what they are saying but the way they are saying it. We have to listen and hear with every fibre of our beings.

I share with you some thoughts of other people on the subject: Edwin Booth, a nineteenth century American actor remarked, "When you are older you will understand how precious little things, seemingly of no value in themselves, can be loved and prized above all price when they convey the thoughtfulness of a good heart." When my mother came to live with us, she was 85, and her bedroom was tiny. She lived with us for thirteen years. As time went on, she couldn't join us for meals or literally get downstairs, so she spent the last five years of her life in that tiny room. One day I remarked, "Do you want to move into a larger bedroom?" and added, "I would hate to live all day in such a tiny room." "No" she said. "As you get older you value the cosiness of a small room, and your needs are less."

When she developed cataracts, we took her to hospital to have them removed. The surgeon normally removed them one at a time, and as we were seated in the waiting room, Ken, then my mother in a wheelchair, and then me, she asked, "I wonder if he can do both together." The consultant arrived, and we asked the question, and I well remember him looking at the three of us sitting in a row, and saying, "It is a bit epic, isn't it?" and off she went and had both cataracts removed and as we drove home, she was so thrilled to see all the spring flowers and the beauty of the countryside, which she had not been able to see for years. What a thrill!" Daffodils, crocus; she loved Spring, and said, "when I see new growth, I know that God has not forgotten us." I said, "I think that is quite profound."

We had a gentleman at Dean Row Chapel who was a calligrapher, who set that quotation down in his beautiful handwriting with Spring flowers surrounding it, put it into a simple frame and gave it to her. She was delighted.

I came across this little gem of wisdom by a contemporary American preacher and broadcaster, Terry McAuliffe: "Someone who lies about the little things will lie about the big things too." It might be said that lying becomes a way of life for some people, and you and I never know whether what they are telling us is true. How can we? Sometimes they lie to protect themselves, sometimes because they want to present us with the best picture of the situation. We see this most particularly with people in the public arena, and each of us can pinpoint instances, but it is something for all of us to be aware of. "Your sins will find you out" is a well- known dictum. Our personal lives are often other people's property, particularly if we are leaders in our organisations. I recall having told young Ministers at a valedictory service to remember that they live in a goldfish bowl, in the public gaze. When I was Minister at Lye near Stourbridge a woman noticed a pushchair outside the door of the parsonage and wondered whether that indicated that I was married with a child, or even not married with a child. We live in communities, and sometimes we feel we are other people's property.

It is so often the little things, the details of our lives that undermine and colour the larger issues. "Every day, we have plenty of opportunities to get angry, stressed or offended, but what we are doing when we indulge these negative emotions is giving something outside ourselves power over our happiness. We can choose not to let these little things upset us." (words of American preacher, Joel Osteen). We know that these little niggles act like a cancer and eat away inside us, but again, having had opportunities to share these little upsets, can we put them in perspective, deal with them, and then let them go?

So, what really matters?
In the words of Michael Josephson:
Living a life that matters doesn't happen by accident.
It is not a matter of circumstance but of choice.
<u>So, what will matter? How will the value of your days be measured?</u>

What will matter is not what you bought, but what you built; not what you got, but what you gave.
What will matter is not your success, but your significance.
What will matter is every act of integrity, compassion, courage or sacrifice that enriched, empowered, or encouraged others.
What will matter is not your competence, but your character.
What will matter is not how many people you knew, but how many will feel a lasting loss when you are gone.
What will matter are not your memories, but the memories that live in those who loved you.
Living a life that matters doesn't happen by accident.
It is not a matter of circumstance but of choice.
<u>Choose a life that matters.</u>"

Finally, I refer you to the words by an American writer, Bruce Marshall,
"Our lives are made up of small moments,
sharing a meal with friends or family,
wondering about a question that puzzles us,
giving help to another, listening to a person and being listened to,
talking with another about something that makes us sad, an embrace, a smile, a touch, offering a thought that might help, just a little, to make sense of it all".

Our gathering here is just one small moment. It is a small thing we do in gathering together. Yet it is significant.

We can all look to our own experiences, dredge up our own individual memories, add them to those I have highlighted. Large and small matters go hand in hand, and with Dr. Harry Lismer Short, who crafted one of our prayers today, pray, O God of the infinitely small and the infinitely great, dwell in our hearts and lives, to give them meaning at this moment and in eternity. It is then that we learn to see The Robin - tiny though it is, can be more important than the larger objects in the picture, even more important than the little girl, because the robin is the focal point, and the princes in the tower pale into insignificance beside the exquisitely executed life-like painting of what we might be tempted to call the smaller objects, the little details. May we appreciate both the great and small, and not close our eyes to either. Amen

Penny Johnson

PARABLES OF EXPERIENCE

One of the most attractive features about Jesus' teaching is that it reaches every one of us. Older people, who are well versed in New Testament theology, can apply the principles of Jesus' teaching to their own situations. The young can enjoy the stories, for instance, of the lost sheep, or the lost coin, or the Good Samaritan, or the Prodigal Son, to name but four, at their own level of experience. When we tell stories to children, we tend to clothe them with a few more details than are actually given within the pages of the New Testament.

For example, I have told the story of the lost sheep in two ways. One is of the little lost lamb called Snowy who left his mother's side and became stranded on a mountain top. She was beside herself with worry and went in search of him and found him, ticking him off for leaving the fold without permission. He deserves all he got, and yet, naturally she was delighted to have him back. And then, reversed, from Snowy's point of view, cold, hungry, wishing he had done as he had been told. How sorry he was now that he had strayed away. He had been told often enough to stay with the others and now maybe he would die of cold on the rocky hillside.

Likewise, the Good Samaritan. I suppose many people wishing to revive interest in a familiar tale have told the story from the viewpoint of the dying man, embroidering the gory details slightly, with pools of blood around him and hoping someone would come quickly to rescue him. Hope arises within him as he sees, firstly a priest and then a Levite; surely, they will help him, but no, they ignore him and then when all hope has gone, he hears a third set of footsteps - this time the footsteps of someone who will certainly not help - the Samaritan, because Jews and Samaritans hate each other. We put our own flesh around the bones of the story. Jesus himself told these stories in a pithy fashion, such as, "what man of you, having a hundred sheep, if he loses one of them leaves the ninety and nine in the wilderness, and goes after that which is lost, until he finds it, and when he hath found it he layeth it on his shoulders rejoicing". In order to bring understanding and meaning to the parables I believe the essentials need to be expanded and we will all do that in slightly different ways. Much depends on what we hope to get out of the story, what point in the story is important to us? We might see many meanings within them, related to our own experience. They are not finite, they have no final meaning, there are a variety of meanings within them, and we can use the same story to express any one of them.

Take the parable of the prodigal son. The younger son wants his inheritance before his father's death. Let me have it now," he says. Father agrees. Off he goes and squanders it all, returning with nothing, having had a marvellous time and returns, expecting to find nothing had changed from when he went away. One truth is that we can't do that. People change, so that your elder brother who was quite happy to share things with you before you went away, decides quite definitely he is not going to put up with a brother who only considers himself and no-one else. While his younger brother has been making a mess of his life, he has kept things going at home. It's surely expecting a shade too much for him to welcome him back just as though nothing has happened. This worthless individual has come back to plague him and take all his father's affection. Shouldn't the celebration be for him, the elder brother, who has stayed at home and managed the farm? What injustice, and as for father, well, who would have believed that father could have been so stupid as not to have seen through his brother's intention of twisting father round his little finger. So, you can see that I have put a lot of flesh on to the bones of the story which are just not there but might reasonably be so. I have not made the point, which Jesus did, that father celebrated because his son was back amongst them. The implication is, as with all of Jesus's parables, that God cares for everyone, even the prodigal, the reckless, the wasteful and the extravagant. Jesus' point was that there is room for every lost person within the Kingdom of God, for the repentant and those who change their ways.

When teachers are being trained to teach the parables, they are specifically instructed not to point out the moral. Firstly, because children should find their own truths within them and secondly, because the truth of the Kingdom of Heaven, will never be understood by children under the age of twelve. Children have very little concept of "Spirit," "God as Spirit"," Death" and Eternal Life and of a Spiritual Realm, of a Kingdom within the heart and mind.

All that comes later as they mature, and as they experience the spiritual dimensions of life. But they will understand about caring for each other, that no one should be left out in the cold and like all of us, they do have some experience of unfairness. Life is not fair. As the elder brother would see it, he can work in a fairly mundane fashion, not wanting anyone to express their gratitude for what he does, and then your younger brother comes home after having spent all his inheritance and in a dire situation, you don't expect him to be well treated; but when the soreness has worn off and when you see that your younger brother isn't so bad after all and, in any case, you have to live with him, you see the wisdom of letting bygones be bygones. Who is suffering? You are because you are still angry. Nothing is to be gained by carrying on like that. If life is to be at least tolerable for the three of you and father must be considered, then you have to give in and make him welcome. Again, friends, you will see that I have draped the story with shrouds of purple material. but what happens I am suggesting, quite strongly, is that the story has more meaning than Jesus gave it. Jesus used it to make the point that everyone who repents comes to God. This story is a reference point, however, for other truths. Start with any family, if a tolerable atmosphere is to prevail, everyone must pull their weight. Relationships are bound to be soured if we fail to consider others. Then another perennial truth is that everyone needs affection. On the other hand, neither should people be taken for granted. After having done the work of two for a number of years, could be somewhat insulted with the well-meant expression of gratitude, "Son, thou art ever with me." A bit thick, but nevertheless we must overcome all those feelings of animosity for family is family and home is home.

The value of the parables is surely that we can identify with the central characters. Jesus' life and teaching concerned ordinary people, the underdogs, the unworthy and forlorn, the unfortunate, such as the woman taken in adultery, perhaps one of the greatest stories in the New Testament. The Scribes and Pharisees brought to Jesus a woman taken in adultery; it was against the law, and they couldn't wait to stone her and kill her. Jesus did not order them to stop. He didn't point out the cruelty of such an action. He appealed to their better nature. He said, "He who is without sin shall cast the first stone." One by one they left the scene. Jesus was able to invoke a change of heart in all those who would have had her stoned. How far we have come? Thankfully, no one in this country is stoned for such behaviour today, albeit we do see hon-our killings among some families living here. But the story can still set us thinking.

None of this would condone her behaviour. We are not given any insight into the reasons for her adultery. Perhaps that would make a difference to our response. We do, however, respond to the hu-manitarian approach, whatever the sin.

Ultimately, understanding is a far better approach than violence. I personally value the lack of detail in Jesus' parables. They allow us to clothe them with something from our own experience. Instead of being merely a guide as to how we ought to treat our neighbour, they form a framework for our thinking. It is almost as though Jesus presented an idea, and we give it its meaning. Instead, there-fore, of beginning with the parable, or the framework, and then painting it with our experience, we can turn it round. Experience comes first. Be it the joy of finding something which was lost, an earring perhaps, that we felt we would never see again, or having a rotten time with unsympathetic neighbours, or younger member of the family who doesn't fit in with the rest of us, but with a need for understanding and tolerance if life is to proceed happily.

There is a story by David Kossoff about a boy who goes into a small village and is amazed to see three targets set side by side. There is a hole in the middle of each one where the bullet has hit the bullseye. The poor boy, who could not read or write, respon-sible for this feat suddenly appeared, and the young graduate in musketry, addressed him. "how did you do that?," he asked. I have been trying to aim for the bullseye for years, it is, often impossible, but you have done it three times. "look, each one is bang in the middle of the circle. It's miraculous." "That's easy" the marksman replied. "what I do is aim first, then I draw a chalk circle round the hole. Nothing to it." the graduate in marksmanship was absolutely stunned.

That is what Jesus did when he told stories. He told a parable that left the understanding of it to us. It has a meaning for us. Individu-ally, we bring our own experience to it. We find our own truth. Jesus shot the bullets; we draw our own chalk circles around them with our particular insight.

Parables allow us to interpret and reinterpret truths as we see them, and to keep on finding new truths again and again, all through life. These parables are ageless. they have stood the test

of time for over 2000 years because they are about universal and eternal matters of life and death and humanity which are the same from age to age and always will be. Amen.
Penny Johnson

ON DETERMINATION

Sowing Peaches

On the back cover of Carl Scovel's book Never Far from Home. (Stories from the Radio pulpit) his reviewer, Peter J. Gomes writes "Carl Scovel was one of Boston's great preachers and radio's most reassuring voices. He sustained a ministry far beyond the walls of historic King's Chapel, Boston Mass. U.S.A."

In one of the radio broadcasts set out in the book, Scovel relates the following story about his daughter:

"She must have been four or five years old that summer afternoon when Faith and I were planting in the garden, and she had just finished eating a juicy, dripping peach. She came to me with the stone and said, "Daddy, I want to plant this." I looked dubiously at the candidate for resurrection, and with a wisdom born of too many disappointments, I said, "You can plant that, honey, if you want to, but you know it probably won't come up." "But I want to plant it" she said, and I replied, "Okay honey, but remember what I said."

That was over twenty years ago, and last Saturday afternoon I picked up 427 small peaches beneath the tree that sprang from that single stone and now shades a large portion of the back yard, and there must be another 427 peaches still on the tree. They aren't much to eat, but our last sexton made a very decent jam out of them. **So much for the wisdom born of disappointment."**

Unless we are the sort of people who are brilliant at whatever we choose to undertake, and never fail at anything, the chances are that from time to time we shall need to be reminded that we should not be put off by failure and try and try again until we succeed. Whatever we undertake in life, there are bound to be people who are more skilful than we are, and we should look to them for encouragement rather than be daunted by their success.

There is something to be said for "struggle". Even if we don't achieve great heights, to reach our own goals is important. It is difficult not to keep comparing ourselves with those more talented, not to feel diminished by them, but equally important to keep improving, keep working, keep up the momentum, and obtain some satisfaction from our own performance. AND VERY IMPORTANTLY NOT TO BE PUT OFF BY THOSE AROUND US WHO HAVE TRIED IT ALL BEFORE, AND FAILED.

Faith's father prepared her for the worst: it probably wouldn't work. She might have stopped right there, but she didn't. She planted it, and although it looked an unlikely candidate for resurrection, twenty years later there were 427 peaches on the tree. I was reminded of all sorts of occasions in my own life when discouraging voices have warned against taking the first step.

In 1959 a few of us at our Wolverhampton church, decided to start a Sunday School. There had been one until the second world war broke out, and it had been disbanded during wartime. "Why don't you wait until we have young people in the congregation?" some asked. We said, "We want to create one for when there are children." So, we met for weeks and weeks together, as adults, and prepared the ground for a Sunday School. We prepared lessons, bought books, and we canvassed in the area. "We have done all that before" said certain doubtful people. "We have visited people in the neighbourhood and leafleted. It didn't work." But we did it anyway. One week, we had our first child, and before long children who normally played in the park nearby decided to visit us. I tremble now as I think of our publicity, "Bring a friend and score a point." We had a huge sheet on a board, and whenever a child brought along a friend, we gave them a star next to their name on the sheet, and whoever scored the most points won a Golden Treasury of the Bible. Ten years later it became "The Sunday

Group" with no adult leader at all. By this time, I had moved to Oxford to train for the ministry and received a letter from them to say they were disbanding now that they had left school and were going their separate ways in the world. By then they were seventeen! Incidentally, many years later a friend and co-Teacher, Vicky Griffiths met one of the "children" on the bus. Who was then sixty-six but had never forgotten the happy times they'd had. "We loved coming to Sunday School!" she recalled.

How many of us have failed our driving test? What did we do next? Try again, or simply give up? We shall all have our own stories. I passed at my fourth attempt. I decided that all the other tests I had taken were simply wasted if in the end I didn't get through. All the money I had spent so far would have been for nothing. It is easy to remember that incredible reverse, or the emergency stop that wasn't quite soon enough, the nerves that got in the way: I had one examiner who only spoke up at all when the reverse didn't quite work out and I ended up on the other side of the road; and another who held my hand to steady my nerves and allowed me to start again, but failed me because it was I who had to be in charge of the car. IN THE END WE WANT TO PASS THE TEST, DRIVE OUR CAR ON THE ROAD, PUT BEHIND US PAST MISTAKES AND ENJOY DRIVING. That is what I did.

Our School Motto means more to me now than it ever did at school. It is so true, "Vincit qui patitur". "He shall conquer who endures". However, you interpret this: "don't give up." "Keep going until you succeed," "commit yourself to your goal and make great effort"; "keep your nose to the grindstone" "keep going in the difficult times"; "nil desperandum"; it says, in many ways, without commitment and endurance, we shall not succeed. Success is not always to the most talented, it is to those who take pains. In fact, that is one definition of "genius". I am sure there are others, but one at least is the capacity to take pains.

Success is marked by that old adage, "if at first you don't succeed, try, try, try again. Sir Ranulph Fiennes conquered Everest at his third attempt. After reaching the summit he said he felt dreadful. Six years before, he failed because he had a heart problem, which resulted in a triple bypass, and, not wanting to be defeated, he had another go at it. What struck me as very poignant was his philosophy for achieving his goal: "Imagine it is a mountain with no top – don't look up, just endlessly repeat 'plod forever, plod forever'".

Many of us are plodders rather than highflyers. We might belittle our poor attempts. The secret perhaps is not to compare ourselves with others who never fail and can always be relied upon to produce a perfect rendition or performance, (that can be soul destroying). Such achievements can make us want to give up NOW - but compare our own performances now with what they were like a little while ago!

Should we ever give in, or give up? For the last twenty-five years I have played the French horn. I took it up when I realised that I was never going to be another Yehudi Menhuin. I decided that since I had reached my personal limit on the violin, there was still a lot of music inside me that needed an instrument to enable it to come out, and the horn was probably the right choice of instrument for me. The horn is not the easiest of instruments to play. It requires a good deal of breath control, stamina, use of diaphragm and a good firm embouchure, and when you start playing the horn at forty-one, the development of all these skills can take years. If you are a young musician, especially if you are musically gifted, the sky is the limit, success before you, on the concert platform at the age of ten, winner of the young musician of the year at the age of 12, with recording contracts to follow. At least that is the scenario as it appears to me. A friend, Sue Evans and I attended the final of the Young Musician of the Year some years ago. The four finalists were brilliant musicians. They had played a number of instruments in their short lifetimes, and came from musical families, with parents either teaching music or in the recording industry. My friend turned to me and said, "You know what our problem is, Penny: we have the wrong parents." For my part I struggle with my scales, with my pieces, I am nervous about playing in public, and worry endlessly about playing any solos that I might have to play in orchestral or band music. Taking exams is a nightmare, with nerves creeping in, clamminess of hands, and inability to remember a simple tune when played on the piano for me to sing or clap the rhythm, which is part of any examination. Why do I put myself through this, I ask? If I ever take another exam, it will be the last. May be even now, that point has been reached. Why not give the horn up? (orchestra and band also?). Because something inside me says, "hold on", "have faith in yourself", "know that you can succeed, know that commitment, practise, will power and determination all play their part." To give up now is not an option. In fact, I have made quite a bold decision, to play the Mozart Eb Quintet for Horn, violin and two violas at our next Unitarian Music Society Conference at the end of August. That is a goal, and I will do it, but I know that a really conscious effort to play what is an extremely difficult piece, even for professionals, is probably a step too far! However, there must be no backing out. I have told all concerned, they all have their parts, and it is on the programme.

I have always been willing to "have a go" at things. The idea that I may be merely mediocre has never been a reason for my giving up; it may be to others, particularly the conductors of the band and orchestra in which I play, but not to me. Naturally, I would rather be excellent, but I don't give up merely because I am not. I feel sad that "winning" and "being the best" are so important to some people, and that they therefore never have the chance of the learning curve which failure so often brings. I have recently been watching the film, "Chariots of Fire" which features the sportsmen, Harold Abrahams, and Eric Liddell. The Master of Caius College Cambridge encourages all students to do their best. "Let each of you discover where your true chance of greatness lies. Seize this chance, rejoice in it and let no power of persuasion deter you in your task." In the film at least, when Harold Abrahams sees how fast Eric Liddell runs, he is put off the idea of racing at all, and says to his girlfriend, "I run to win. If I don't win, I don't run." And she replied, "If you don't run, you won't win." Quite. So, encouraged by her, he embarks on further training, which makes all the difference, of course, and gives him the power to succeed. What are we afraid of? A young woman I know is so afraid of not reaching perfection that she cannot make a start on projects. That may be the case for others also. My own solution is "make a start somehow and somewhere. Don't waste time worrying. Correct and amend as you go." As it happens both Harold Abrahams and Eric Liddell won their races at the Olympic Games, and were renowned for their excellence, but that had not been achieved without its pain, exercises, a great deal of training, and mixed emotions. In the film Harold Abrahams says of the race, "I had been in fear of losing, now I am almost too frightened to win." Quite a dilemma! I cite Thomas Huxley's words, "Perhaps the most valuable result of all education is the ability to make yourself do the thing you have to do, when it ought to be done, whether you like it or not. It is the first lesson that ought to be learned. That must apply to leisure and relaxation as well as having one's nose to the grindstone."

So often the line between success and failure is so fine that we scarcely know when we pass it. How many people with a little more patience, and a little more willpower, a little more perseverance and commitment, would have succeeded. How sad, then, not to put the final spring in the step, the final burst of energy into a project, the final touches to make a dream come true. How important is perseverance and will-power?

For some years now I have visited a woman who is "one brave little lady." I conducted her wedding in the early eighties. She has had a very unfortunate hand of cards dealt to her throughout her life and has lurched from crisis to crisis for many years. As a child she was involved in an accident, and as a result, suffered hip and leg problems, with abscesses in her bones, and by extension, blood poisoning, and therefore, much immobility, but always cheerful with a love of life, an independent spirit, a thirst for knowledge and a real positive attitude, and great sense of fun. Never ever did

I hear her say, "why me?" or lament her lot in life. She loved to go to her writing class, and we had endless discussions on religion. Her marriage had been breaking up, almost from the beginning, and her husband left her without any warning at a poignant time, when she was diagnosed with motor neurone disease, and needed him most. During this time, she wrote a book of fifty-six short stories, which was published one week before she died. I am full of admiration for her. What a triumph. What determination. I look at her and think, "Would I have been as strong and tolerant of people who let me down, as she?" I have never seen greater fortitude than hers - ever.

He shall conquer who endures. I have always understood this to mean, "he or she takes pains", "suffers" doesn't give in at the first or second hurdles. Having put one's hand to the plough, don't look back." These are familiar sayings. Another is "no short cuts, don't be so busy learning the tricks that you never learn the trade."
Life is not a rehearsal.

I conclude with some words by a good friend of mine who has just celebrated his hundredth birthday. His name is John Mellor, and he is a member of the Kidderminster congregation, and a wonderful artist. This is what he wrote in the latest calendar of Unitarian New Meeting House, Kidderminster, called "The Record".

"WOW! Yes. I've made my first hundred and, like Geoffrey Boycott, my mind is set on increasing the figure. Think positive and the score will increase. It's the effort all along the way, and if the pitch is occasionally bumpy, play it carefully and the score will increase. Share the joy of your first hundred with many spectators and the world will be a much happier place." The sentiments belong to John, but the spirit is an inspiration to all who seize life and make things happen, who put their hands to the plough and never look back. Amen

Penny Johnson

THE PRIESTHOOD OF ALL BELIEVERS "MORNING FATHER"

Our butcher had a great sense of humour: you could always rely on him for the wise crack, the merry quip, and keeping the customers rolling in the aisles, and one busy Saturday morning I joined the end of the queue, which was as long as it could possibly be without extending outside on to the pavement, and as I stood there, he looked at me and said, "Morning Father". All eyes then turned, and I smiled an embarrassed smile. It had all the makings of a sketch by Victoria Wood. It didn't seem to be the right moment to say, "But I am not a Father. In fact, I'm not a priest at all." "No Bishop had laid his hands upon me and connected me in some mysterious way with St. Peter and the Apostles. I do not carry the kind of authority of a Priest". In fact, had I said all that it would have been totally out of place and lacking good humour and would have held no interest at all for the butcher or for his customers whose dearest wish was to get to the front of the queue for their joint or chops or bacon and sausages, and so I remained silent. As you may know, there is a distinction between a Priest, whose authority for ministry comes from God because a Bishop lays his hands upon his head, and he is made aware that he is in direct line of succession from St. Peter - and our own Ministers, whose authority for Ministry comes from the congregation that he or she serves.

Whereas a Bishop transfers spiritual insight and spiritual gifts to Priests, so enabling them to carry out their ministries to their people, we start the other way round. Our Ministers are not thought to be especially spiritually endowed. There is no laying on of hands, and certainly there is no thought that a Minister is more able to communicate with God than a lay person. Religious insight, and indeed the whole dimension of life which we call broadly "religious" is available to all of us. There is no distinction. It is the quality of life and living that is important, not the priestly robes. We believe that we are all capable of becoming instruments of God and can reach God (or some might say a higher power) without any intermediary figure, be it Jesus, Peter, Paul, or a Priest. In that sense we acknowledge the wisdom of that great figure of the Reformation, Martin Luther, who claimed that **"There is a Priesthood of all believers". Insight and belief and spirituality are not given to a few chosen people only, but are available to all.** We might say that we all have a direct link with the Holy Spirit... none of us is set apart.

However, it helps when we are organising our worship to have a key figure whose task it is to be sensitive to the spiritual needs of our individual communities, who has been given authority to organise worship. We, the people, give to our chosen minister or lay leader the authority to minister to us. For us, it not enough for the religious leader to have a title. It is not the Office that we revere. Respect is not given because that person is a trained minister carrying the courtesy title of Reverend. Respect has to be earned. Ministry only really works when we respect each other, and Respect should be mutual. We value each other.

That, of course, is a view of Ministry from one side only, there will be some church members who attribute far more power to their minister than the minister might be happy with. Ministers don't have magic wands, but they might well have healing power, or enable someone to come to terms with their own situation, or initiate prayer, or help someone to hold on when holding on is almost impossible, and, when all the other agencies of help have been unable to find a solution, "to be there" to make a difference. Lay people may also possess healing power.

For some people, their Minister may be the nearest thing to God that they have. If someone is placing all their faith in their Minister, it is probably not the best idea to pull the mat from under them.

It is such a privilege to share other people's deepest moments and bring something of that divinity we call God to their situation. On the whole, a person with a need doesn't stop to distinguish between a Lay Leader, Minister or Priest. He or she is looking for guidance, inspiration, and a way forward. Because of the nature of our own non-conformist position, we have never assumed special powers for our Ministers. Divinity resides within us all be we minister or lay. Some lay people are rather better than ministers at particular and special kinds of support.

This church operates more fully because it values the worth and significance of the gifts of everyone in it, and the capacity for developing spiritually. In the sense that we are all open to the spiritual revelation of the divine, and channels through which divinity is radiated and spread, we are all ministers of the divine. This might be a surprise to us. It shouldn't be! We all communicate holiness. It is not the privilege of trained Ministers only.

I was once invited to the home of a Bishop for lunch. I believe it was the Bishop's wife who actually invited me. His name was Richard Hanson. He had been a Bishop in Ireland some little time before and was, when I met him, a Professor at Manchester University. He had a brother who was also an Anglican Priest. Fairly naturally I suppose, I wondered whether I would be able to "hold my own" in any discussion, and very nervously rang the doorbell. He was wonderful. I was at ease immediately. "Are you a Priest?" he asked me in the course of conversation. "No" I said, "I'm a Minister. He pursued the line of enquiry. "Do you feel that you are a channel between God and your people?" "Yes" I said, without hesitation. "Then" he said, "You are a Priest." Having thought about this, I should have added that surely that would also apply to a lay person. In my estimation, it certainly would.

It is a bit like St. Paul preaching so eloquently of the many gifts that come to the fore in Ministry, that if used wisely make the church great...the gift of tongues, those with miraculous powers, the healers, the helpers, who give of their time and experience for the good of all. We think of medical practitioners, psychologists, psychotherapists, osteopaths, divine healers. "You are the temple of God" he said. We know that the power of spiritual life comes from "doing". I am a firm believer in divine healing, having personally experienced it. This was from God, through the Rev. Joyce Hazlehurst, a Unitarian Minister, who asked me to pray with her for strength and guidance so that the healing power would reach me. She came to a Discussion Group I held at the Manse, and I went out of the room to prepare refreshments, and when I returned there was no Joyce and no one else either. They were all in a queue up the stairs waiting for their turn to be healed. We preach, if you like, by the way we minister to one another. Which is testimony to the friar preacher who was dying to preach in the traditional way, only to be told that real preaching is a way of life. We are all Instruments of God, and any one of us could be chosen as a special instrument at any time.

My own personal experience of God which has informed my faith in a power beyond myself came in 1974 when I was a student for the Ministry, and I was working with the Rev. Andrew Hill at Ullet Road Church, in Liverpool during the Christmas vacation. I was due to conduct a service at Gateacre Chapel, and knew no one there at all. I had previously discovered that the niece of one of the Chapel officers had been killed in a hijacking of a Pan Am Airline when terrorists had shot randomly around on the plane. The Chapel Officer explained to me that she was awaiting news of the niece's husband, the pilot of the plane. He was missing. Had I decided to mention any of this to the congregation, I would have done so through prayer, but this was not my news to share. I was a visitor. At that time, I could not liberate myself from notes. Every word of the sermon had to be read. Extempore preaching was not an option!

Very suddenly and quite unexpectedly in the middle of the Christmas sermon concerning shepherds, kings, a baby, and a star, I found myself speaking about tragedy at Christmas time. It was as though I had been taken over by a power which was not my own, and enabled to speak more eloquently than I have done before or since. I do remember coming back to earth and finding the last page of the sermon and finishing it off in the usual way. At the door, while greeting the congregation a man came up to me and said: "Thank you for the sermon this morning. I found it enormously helpful. You see I lost my wife this week in an aeroplane disaster. I am the pilot of the plane." From that day, the words, "Lord, make me an instrument of thy peace" have taken on a more profound and personal meaning. We can all be instruments of God.

Within our churches we have dedicated men and women who devote much of their lives to carrying out a ministry. Most of them have weekday jobs, and then at the weekends they contribute to the activities of Sunday Schools and lead services of worship, and without them many of our churches would have closed long ago. They spend hours making preparations for church and chapel services. I ran a Sunday School at Wolverhampton for many years and was a lay preacher for nine. My father was a lay preacher for fifty years or more, taking funerals and christenings also, like many of his generation. The spiritual life is in the hands of us all, lay and minister alike.

In that we all, in various ways, channel divinity to each other, we are those designated by Martin Luther as the Priesthood of all believers, and in the eyes of the Anglican Bishop, Richard Hanson we are **all** Priests. There is a hymn in one of our older hymn books used for Induction Services by W. C. Gannett, which rather makes the point:O not to one, but all, our God,

Grant ordination free,
To heights of life as yet untrod,
And nobler ministry.

To tenderer words, to braver deeds,
To wills set fast in right,
To heartbeats rhymed to other's needs,
To love and life and light.

Ordain in all the seeker's mind
Of eager, trusting youth,
That hurries forth each morn to find
New manna-falls of truth.

Ordain the prophet-heart that takes
Lone sides with outcast worth:
Ordain the helping hand that makes
A dawn of heaven on earth.
Amen

Penny Johnson

THE JOY OF LIVING

Wherever we live, whatever communities we belong to, there are some things common to all of us. These things are independent of wealth, background, education, and social status. Two of the things that I have found common to everyone at some point in life are Joy and Sorrow. Very often we find our deepest experiences in our joy and sorrow for the two are closely related and at times it is nigh impossible to separate them.

Within every person there will be times when you become depressed or plain fed up - a mountain of work to be done, bills to be paid, gardens and houses to be maintained, meals to be prepared. In all our lives we can remember times like that, and one clearly stands out in

my memory from 1965. We were in College on a Thursday evening and I had some Greek to prepare for an exam the next day. My feelings at that time were like those that my own children felt when they faced exams; I felt like walking out on the lot, a black cloud of depression descended. After dinner I went into the Common Room and picked up the Manchester Evening News. There on the front page I saw a letter entitled, "Thank you for the precious gift of life." It was from a girl in the Hulme area of Manchester. At that time, the whole area was devastated through so called slum clearance and wherever that girl lived in Hulme she must have overlooked destruction and desolation. Listen though to what she wrote: - "It's only an ordinary day, yet I feel so happy and I have just realised how precious life is... I thought how good it feels to be alive." Then she continued, "Some people are less fortunate than others in many ways, but God gave to everybody many ways of showing happiness... A smile, a soft, pure smile." Her letter ended by giving thanks for the most precious gift of life."

The writer was Maureen Rhodes, a 16 year old Catholic girl and Maureen had captured the real Joy of Living in an area where there was much sorrow and misery.

Of course, if we are cynical we might say, "Ah well, I was like that at 16 with a long life to look forward to, perhaps she had just made a date with her first boy-friend or started a good new job. They would be good reasons for being full of the Joy of Living. - I remember it well."

We can say that, but I still suggest that at any age we can experience this joy of Living. I've seen elderly people light up with joy as they return home after a stay in hospital or even after a holiday, and again I return from one of those vivid memories that we all have from long ago. This memory came well after the Manchester experience, from my days in London.

During a Christmas holiday I went to see a great aunt in a hospital near Salisbury. Aunt Polly was then 87 with a husband of the same age, both had been suspicious of doctors and hospitals and had thankfully enjoyed good health. Throughout their married life the couple had never been parted. Just before Christmas my aunt fractured a hip and was taken to Odstock Hospital, her family thought she would never pull through, partly through her age and partly through the enforced separation. At first, she was miserable especially when they told her that Christmas would have to be spent in hospital. Then there was a change, it's hard to say what caused it - perhaps it was the devotion of the doctors and nurses. Whatever it was my aunt discovered a whole new world of experience. In the hospital she met people that she would never have met within her own little village of Porton; aunt discovered that doctors and nurses weren't so bad after all - that even at 87 years of age her treatment was as good as that given to teenagers on the same ward.

Her stay in hospital showed her some of the kindness that existed in the wider world and it brought her whole family closer together. When I visited she was in a room called "Daily Living", it was a rehabilitation centre and my aunt was learning to walk again. To teach her, a Zimmer frame was used - then in its early days. Amongst the people there was a great sense of achievement when they walked a few extra steps. It was amazing to see my aunt with an Anglican cum Baptist background betting an old three-pence (about one and a half pence today) against a young lad injured in a motor cycle accident that she would walk an extra three steps that day - a penny a step! Each day they placed bets on who could walk the furthest.

At the age of 87 aunt re-discovered the joy of living - and she rediscovered it through her initial suffering. When aunt returned home the experience in hospital became a talking point for the rest of her life.

From a 16 year old Mancunian to an 87 year old lady in Wiltshire. What about all of us in between? Katharine Whitehorn in the Observer has been one of my favourite writers over the years and in one article she wrote a piece called "A fine time to be alive" People had been harking back to the good old days and telling her how of how little progress had really been made. Katharine looks at progress in a practical way and comments: -

"Dirty nappies are dirty nappies in any age but today more people have washing machines and disposable nappies. Modern medicine has helped me to survive acute appendicitis, fifty years ago I would have died. The figures for many hobbies are on the increase, there is a shorter working week; in retirement many people can actually enjoy their leisure. There is an increase in the social conscience, Oxfam, Save the Children Fund etc."

In conclusion Katherine Whitehorn added that whatever is wrong with our society it will NOT be put right by looking back to a golden age that never existed. This is a fine time to be alive. It is a time to experience the joy of living. How right she is, at one of my churches the burial register records that in the late 1700s a whole generation of children died of smallpox – they were certainly not the good old days. As I write, a Covid virus has been raging but with modern medicine and vaccines many lives have been saved, unlike those poor children long ago.

The significance in the experience of the girl in Manchester, my elderly aunt and Katharine Whitehorn can be seen in the words of John's Gospel. "My joy I give unto you and your joy no man taketh from you." In all the experiences of life we can still find some joy, a joy which no one can take from us. As the Baptist Harry Emerson Fosdick put it, "Jesus could stand anything that men or circumstances could do to him and still have resources of joy."

Centuries after John, the Arab Christian mystic Kahlil Gibran put it even better in his book, "The Prophet" when he wrote,

"Your joy is your sorrow unmasked. And the self-same well from which your laughter rises were oftentimes filled with your tears... When you are joyous, look deep into your heart and you shall find it is only that which has given you sorrow that is giving you joy.

When you are sorrowful, look again in your heart, and you shall see that, in truth you are weeping for that which has been your delight."

Those words are so true for the experience of joy often comes to us through sorrow, our sorrow often appears after losing something or someone that brought us joy. Through all of life the joy of living can still be part of our lives and often in the most unexpected ways - a visit from an old friend, a bunch of dandelions in the hand of a child, in our own gardens and homes, in hearing a familiar voice on the radio, in the strains of both triumphant and quiet music, a well-loved song, or even a new work that we like.

A good religious faith should constantly remind us that life is worth living, that joy and sorrow are intermingled, that life isn't always easy but we can find some joy. Years ago I read a book by a Unitarian Minister, Arnold Lewis called "The Friendly Church" and he wrote: -

"The Friendly Church makes possible the freest sort of interchange of gifts, without invidious comparisons or contrasts. In it no one will be branded, nor haloed, they will be treated with respectful sincerity. In such a company, success would not engender pride, nor disappointment lapse into despair."

A hymn we often use has words to express this joy of living; the joy of a girl in Manchester, of an 87 year old in hospital; of a writer in the Observer. The music is some of Beethoven's finest and the words are by an American Presbyterian. Beethoven was almost stone deaf when he wrote the Ninth Symphony yet he was convinced that the spirit of people could triumph over all the sadness--if that spirit was supported by an inner strength. This is one verse from that hymn.

> "Ever singing march we onward,
> Victors in the midst of strife;
> Joyful music lifts us sunward
> In the triumph song of life."

May we all somehow, find the Joy of Living, the joy that no one can take from us.

Peter Hewis

MESSAGES FOR HUMANS

Several years ago, the telephone rang, and it was my wife's sister from Hong Kong asking if we could have their Jack Russell dog Jasper for two weeks after he came out of quarantine, just until they found a house in Britain. Jasper came out of quarantine looking like a bag of bones and was very unhappy. We were given twenty pounds to cover the cost of dog food and possibly a visit to the vet. Guess what happened then! Jasper stayed for nine years and shared his life with us; he felt secure in our home and gained his normal weight. Furthermore, he became part of the chapel life and enjoyed bits of cake at all the coffee mornings. Oh, and we only ever had the twenty pounds in the whole nine years! During those years we realized that although we taught Jasper a great deal, he in return taught us a great deal. In my experience people seem to be divided between dog lovers and cat lovers and we are in the former camp. However, in recent years our neighbours have asked us to look after their cats when they go on holiday and during one holiday, we started off with three cats and ended up with eleven after one gave birth to eight kittens. The old matriarch cat, Lucy, was bullied by the younger cats and turned up on our doorstep looking bedraggled and forlorn. With the permission of her owners, we now give her breakfast, but only breakfast and she eats it outside. Furthermore, Lucy has adopted our side of the lane as her territory. In a sense she has become an adopted member of the family although we are not cat lovers.

Why do I tell you these stories?

I tell them because animals have formed an important part in the folklore of every nation and every religion. The Beast-tale or animal tale has regularly been used to teach human beings of universal feelings and emotions. In some respects, the tale of the Owl and the Pussycat was intended to convey some of the absurdity in our lives and so was one of my favourite books, Wind in the Willows, just think of Mr. Toad wanting the latest motor car and of the characters who reflect something of our own lives, Ratty, Mole and Badger. The use of animal tales is manifold, some are simply folklore, others have been told as a form of satire and others have taught eternal truths.

Messages for humans frequently appear in animal fables but only two nations seem to have made regular use of the fables to teach some moral ideas. The earliest literature in Greece and India makes frequent use of fables and the stories were well known amongst the people. In both countries special circumstances raised the fable from folklore into literature.

In Greece during the time of the Tyrants, when free speech was dangerous, the fable was largely used for political purposes. The creator of this usage went by the name of Aesop. Aesop was a slave at Samos his name has now become part of our English language. He used fables as early as 550 BC and when free speech returned to Greece fables continued to be used. Later on, other writers created more fables that have been attributed to Aesop. **In India,** the great ethical reformer Sakyamuni, or Buddha, adapted from Brahmin Hindus the use of the animal tale for moral purposes, he made them into fables. Indian thought included that of transmigration of souls and so an animal fable could be accepted as an anecdote about a man who took the form of a beast. Centuries later the cartoons of the French Revolution appeared using animals to represent leaders of the French government. I wonder what animal cartoon we might use today to represent some of our politicians? Fables are still used today; they have a value and make delightful stories for children. Often, they have a message for human beings, but one would use them sparingly in our society because for some people the Fables of Aesop seem too simple.

Why then might animals still have messages human beings? It is surely through that very simplicity. We all remember the story of the Hare and the Tortoise taking part in a race and the message is that *slow, steady plodding can still win a symbolic race* - is that really too simple a message? I think not. What about the story of Noah's Ark in the Old Testament? *It surely means be prepared for a rainy day!* Is the parable of the one lost sheep in the New Testament still relevant? *The message is that each individual is important,* and I think such stories are still valuable.

My purpose in mentioning animal tales or Fables is to show how the lives of many creatures can still play a part in the lives of human beings. Sometimes it is actual contact with creatures, the sparrow eating the breadcrumbs in our garden, the robin following the garden spade, other species that are dependent upon our feeding them in a harsh winter or providing them with water in a dry summer. We feed them and in return they bless us with their presence and sometimes their song, that is a truly Franciscan thought. I know that members of this congregation have cats and dogs, perhaps there are other pets: in previous congregations I have known members with budgerigars, tropical fish, gerbils, guinea pigs, racing pigeons and even stick insects.

The universality of animal life has led to international stories like Brer Rabbit in America, Alice in Wonderland in Oxford, the stories of elephants and cows in India and camels in Egypt. Maybe the stories were written for adults and not for children, written to provide messages for human beings.

How can we learn from such legends and stories? We can learn from them because animal life is close to our lives. St Francis of Assisi found an affinity between animal and human life and showed that in the words we heard earlier, *"Praised be my Lord God with all his creatures."* The scientist Charles Darwin found many messages for humans through his research. On the Galapagos Islands off South America he found giant tortoises, huge lizards, enormous crabs, and sea lions. His discoveries reinforced thoughts on evolution that had already taken shape in his mind. No longer could Darwin accept the thought of a world created in seven days as a credible thought. He no longer thought that every species has been created whole and unchanged throughout the ages. His book "Origin of Species" took shape, suggesting that species of animals face the same circumstances as human beings, famine, disease, death, and accidents. Darwin evolved the doctrine of "natural selection" or the struggle for existence, at times even the survival of the fittest! In numerous cases today artificial selection has taken place, we have selected and bred those animals that are most useful to us, horses to plough and to ride, cows for food and drink, dogs for farm work and protection, cats to catch vermin and pets for companionship. I'm oversimplifying Darwin's theory, but we can see one message for humans from the animal world that Darwin stressed, **the strong survive and the weak perish - unless we support the weak**. It's rather like our neighbour's cat Lucy being bullied and so we try to support her.   Pavlov the psychologist provided another message for humans when he experimented with animals. The message that he provided is that their basic instincts are identical to ours. Those instincts include fear, rage, the eating instinct, the snuggling up and getting warm instinct and then on to the more complicated instincts of curiosity, protectiveness, showing off, companionship, the courting and mating instinct. Pavlov suggested that purely instinctive behaviour is inborn in animals and humans. For twenty-five years he experimented with dogs, the experiments concerned stimulation and inhibition, a form of conditioning. He was able to make a dog drool when a buzzer sounded, simply because the dog had been conditioned into associating the buzzer with food. In contrast he could make a dog frightened on seeing food in a certain kind of dish, which the dog knew would give an electric shock; thus, fear conquered hunger; he even made a dog neurotic.

In the last few years of his life Pavlov discovered that many of the neurotic patients in a mental hospital had symptoms similar to those he had created in the dogs. At least he found a message for humans in his dogs - **our basic instincts are identical.** Albert Schweitzer was helped by the animal world and found a whole outlook on life from his observations of animals, birds, reptiles, and insects. His philosophy was never to needlessly hurt any creature. Reverence for life involves the recognition that all creatures have the will to live and therefore we should respect the will or instinct whenever possible. Here is yet another message for human beings - **we all have a will to live, and we should have reverence for life.**

For some final thoughts on animals and birds I turn to the Austrian naturalist Conrad Lorenz, a man who spent all his life studying living creatures. Lorenz discovered a bird community, which was subtle, well organized and possessed of ritual and mystery – a life far more complex than humans had previously thought possible. The community he found was that of the greylag geese. When a greylag goose loses its mate, it flies around for weeks on end searching for the mate, day, and night its call goes on, gradually it flies further and further afield still crying for the lost partner. When the bird realizes that its mate is not returning the goose loses all courage, it becomes hesitant, frightened, and panicky. The bird's eyes deepen in their sockets, the muscles around the eyes sag and an expression of grief registers on the widowed bird's face. Grief, Lorenz writes, is only one of the emotions we share with animals and birds. Lorenz saw so much of animals and birds in danger and under stress that he became worried about our own species, he draws many parallels with modern life and lists amongst them overcrowding and the perils of urban living. The general loosening of individual and collective responsibility appalled him, and he wrote, *"We should be responsible, a human ought to have their own bit of territory, a house and garden of their own."* **There we see another message for humans - increasing pressure on our territory will bring friction and perhaps even destruction.**

Let's end where I began with Jasper the dog that came for two weeks and stayed for nine years; he gave us and our family a message for human beings, in fact he gave us at least four messages.

1. Support the weak or else they can die.
2. Recognise our own basic needs and instincts.
3. Show reverence for life – for we all have the will to live.
4. Take care of the environment, it is for everyone to enjoy and we only have one world.

Francis of Assisi was so right when he said, "Praised be my Lord God with all his creatures." For those creatures provide many messages for humans.

Peter Hewis

"ASPECTS OF LOVE – BEFORE AND AFTER ANDREW LLOYD WEBBER!"

Week by week people come to places of worship and are surrounded by familiar objects and quotations but how often do we really take them in? In many of our churches and chapels, in fact in churches of all denominations, the word Love appears many times.

Several months ago, I visited a church in Kidderminster and before our visit I looked at their web pages, the pages contain two quotations relevant to my theme. The first reads, "One beautiful world, wrapped in love" and the second quote was, "We are optimistic that love always prevails." I wonder how many of the people in Kidderminster read those words on a regular basis, or look at the words inside their building where they have several memorials mentioning the word "love"?

Once when we were in the Old Meeting House at Mansfield there was some spare time before the service began so I looked around the chapel and found the word "Love" or variations of the word all over the place, especially in the stained-glass windows. To my left the first window had the phrase, "Let us love one another, for love is of God." In the second window was the one word "Love," the third window stated, "Now abideth faith, hope, love, these three and the greatest of these is love." The fourth window mentioned someone of "Beloved memory." On the other side a window had the phrase "Loving memory." Then above a table at the front was the phrase, "Love the Lord thy God, and thy neighbour as thyself." At the end of the service several people told me that even after many years in the chapel they had never read the words but now they would.

"Love" is an amazing word with many meanings, and it changes as we move through life. It probably starts when we are children and have a love of parents and grandparents; likewise, they have a love for us. Then we move on to love of friends, girlfriends or boy-friends, husbands, wives, partners, love of community. There are a few people who even have a love of committees!

Some people even have a love for church notice boards. On pass-ing a church or chapel I'm sure many of you will have seen a notice board with some kind of quotation on it. Some are rather infantile like the words "Ch..ch, What's missing? The answer is UR!" Thank-fully, our Unitarian messages are not like that and we call them Wayside Pulpits. The first Wayside Pulpit in Britain was posted on December 26, 1920 on the notice board of Cross Street Unitar-ian Chapel in Manchester for all of Manchester to see. The first quotation each year is a New Year message from the Lord Mayor of Manchester and then the rest are suggested by chapel members and friends. For many years they were all hand painted by a chapel member. Ever since 1920, a new poster appeared every Sunday morning for a week. Even when Manchester was blitzed during World War II and the Chapel stood roofless, a weekly message ap-peared. People have often been inspired by the words and many of our churches do still use those posters. I've always believed that the Wayside Pulpit is a valuable means of communication. At my previous church in Hinckley a local doctor once said to me, *"You know that I am a humanist, but I love to read your Wayside Pulpits, they are full of common sense and inspiration. Then he added, "Will you conduct my funeral?"* Thankfully, he is still alive and living in Richmond on Thames.

How then can I relate the word love to a Wayside Pulpit? Let's go back over 50 years. The story comes from my first ministry at Mansford Street in Bethnal Green. Our Victorian pile of a church and the parsonage were sandwiched amongst tenement buildings and opposite a Junior School. One evening around 5.30pm I was looking out of the parsonage window and saw a young couple on the opposite side of the street by the school. They were obviously coming home from work and stopped to look across at the church. I watched them for a few minutes and suddenly the man put his arms around the girl, hugged her, kissed her and then they walked off. Wondering what they had been looking at I went outside and looked at the church wall. On the Wayside Pulpit it read, *"If you love someone then tell them before it's too late!"* What a fine thought for all of us and I've often wondered what has happened to that couple.

What aspects of love can we find in our lives? In the Shorter Oxford Dictionary there are many definitions, including, "to entertain, a great regard for, to hold dear, to entertain a strong affection, to be in love, to be devoted or addicted to, to take pleasure in the existence of."

Now I have to apologise to anyone who loves and can speak Greek because, even after I had lived in Cyprus for over two years, my least favourite subject in college was New Testament Greek - but the Greeks can teach us something about the word Love. Going way back in time the Greeks had five words for aspects of love.

EPITHUMIA - (Pronounced: ep-ee-thoo-mee'-ah) - a Greek word for strong desire.

EROS - is their word for passionate romantic love, hence the statue of Eros on Piccadilly in London, he is shooting arrows to make people fall in love. The word erotic comes from this word.

STORGE (Pronounced: stor-ye or stor-ge) - means natural affection, like that felt by normal parents for children or to describe relationships within the family, the love of mother, father, brothers, and sisters.

PHILLIA (Phil-ia)-which means friendship, it includes loyalty to friends, family, and community. The city of Philadelphia gets its name from this word and means the city of brotherly love. This word can apply to our churches, chapels and many voluntary societies, a community.

AGAPE (Pronounced: ah-GAH-pay) - it means a general affection; agape is used to denote feelings for a good meal, your children, and the feelings for a spouse. The word appears in the New Testament describing, amongst other things, the relationship between Jesus and the beloved disciples. In our Oxford chapel we have a painting of the Last Supper that depicts this word. The word is used in the passages "Love your neighbour as yourself," and "This is my commandment, that you love one another as I have loved you." The word even extends to loving your enemies.

Each of those five words represents an aspect of love but that's enough Greek for one day; it never was my favourite subject!

Part of the inspiration for my title came whilst hearing the Mayor of Boston speaking four years ago at the memorial service in April 2013 for those killed at the Boston Marathon. The Mayor, Tom Menino, who had discharged himself from hospital and was helped out of his wheelchair to speak, said this: -

"Since the clocks struck that fateful hour, love has covered this resilient city. I have never loved it and its people more than I do today. We love the brave ones who felt the blast and still raced to the smoke. With ringing in their ears, they tugged gates to the ground to answer cries from those in need. This was the courage of our city at work. We love the fathers and the brothers who took shirts off their backs to stop the bleeding. The mothers and the sisters who cared for the injured. The neighbors and the business owners, the homeowners all across this city, they opened their doors and hearts to the weary and the scared. They said, 'What's mine is yours. We'll get through this together.' This was the compassion of our city at work."

Then he ended with these words: -

"It's a glorious thing, the love and the strength that covers our city.

It will push us forward; it will push thousands and thousands and thousands of people across the finish line next year. Because this is Boston, a city with the courage, compassion and strength that knows no bounds."

Well, that is a fine example of one aspect of love amongst people of all faiths and none in one American city and should apply to all our towns and cities.

Let's go back to my story of the Wayside Pulpit because it applies to so many situations. It would surely appeal to Andrew Lloyd Webber because it was one of the aspects that he depicted in his musical, "Aspects of Love" but he moved beyond that romantic love to include many aspects, to the many forms that love takes. His great hit song, "Love changes everything" might apply to most of our relationships and even mentions, "How you live and how you die." The song ends with the words, "Love will never let you be the same."

Love takes many forms, between couples seeing a Wayside Pulpit, people in a good marriage or relationships, children and parents, grandparents and same sex commitments, human and animal relationships, seeing someone in hospital and suddenly realizing how much they mean to you through the simple love that a good friendship can create. The list could go on, and Lloyd Webber included many of the aspects in his songs. One favourite song seems to give the impression that it was written for a young woman star struck by a man because it has the title, "The first man you remember." In fact, he wrote it to depict a father and daughter and the song is a duet between the father George and his daughter Jenny, it is a father's poem to his daughter.

The Greeks and Andrew Lloyd Webber were so right, there are many aspects of love and all religious traditions stress the importance of love even if evil fanatics ignore them.

We would be wise to go back to the couple in Bethnal Green looking at the Wayside Pulpit, because the words apply to so many situations and we can all heed the advice. ***"If you love someone then tell them before it's too late."*** I could add, "for tomorrow we take the next step of life and love." As life moves on, we all need to remember the words of that Wayside Pulpit as we take our next steps through life.

Think of all your own relationships, then you will sense the many "Aspects of Love" and if you love someone then tell them before it's too late!

Peter Hewis

PRAYERS

FOR FRIENDS

O God, we are so thankful for our friends, real friends whose loyalty is never doubted. Some of them have been with us all our lives. We have grown up with them. We offer support to each other in the good times and the bad. We are "there" for each other, we know each other's thoughts; we do not need words. Words are superfluous.

Blessings come in many forms. Close friendships are some of the finest blessings we have. What a privilege it is to have close friends whom we trust with our most intimate secrets, who struggle with us to find a solution to a tricky problem and who can often throw light on an almost intractable stumbling block, as if by magic.

These are friends with whom we can argue, who may disagree with our point of view, but even though there is disagreement, the friendship remain rock solid. We know that our secrets are safe with them; they will never divulge them or compromise us.

For close friendships that have stood the test of time, we are thankful.

Penny Johnson

WEDDING PRAYER

O God, we bring into this sacred space our deepest moments. Such a moment is this one when two soulmates have become partners for life. They have vowed to take each other in good times and in bad, for better for worse. Life is not always straightforward. It has twists and turns, heights and depths, sorrow and joy, cloudless skies, and muddy patches.

Marriage brings us together quite uniquely. Every marriage is unique. It draws into itself all that is special about the two people most intimately involved. There is not another marriage quite like this one, and there never will be. Uniqueness cannot be copied. There are many aspects of marriage, but central to it all is our commitment to each other.

Penny Johnson

THE STREAM OF LIFE

O God we are thankful for the stream of life which carries us forward to new, amazing happenings. Around a corner we meet unexpected diversions. When we look back at the way we have travelled so far, we may see a pattern forming. We live our lives forward, and it is only when we look back at the way we have come that we can make sense of our journey.

Sometimes it seems that we have been shunted into a siding; our journey has been frustrated. We who feel that we shape our lives by the decisions we take may start to question this belief. It appears that another hand than ours is directing our pathway and that we are no longer in control.

Retrospectively we can see more fully how we fit into the great scheme of things, and how, very gently, this stream of life gets us back on track and redirects our pathway. May we always be thankful.

Penny Johnson

FOR GOOD PARENTS

O God, as children in our formative years we are guided, primarily by our parents. We do not question what they say or do. We simply follow.

Gradually as we gain knowledge and grow in understanding, we find our own voice and act with confidence in ourselves. We become more independent of other people, but the bedrock of principles and values that our parents gave us remain, and we are thankful.

But for their influence and guidance our platform of moral and religious values would be sadly diminished.

As parental ties loosen and we are thrust into the big wide world as independent human beings, we offer our thanks to those who shaped our early lives, thus allowing us to fly freely, and take our place in the world.

Penny Johnson

CHILDREN

"A child's world is fresh and new and beautiful, full of wonder and excitement." * Those of us who have told stories to children have been struck by the light in their eyes, their "hanging on to every word." What a responsibility we have to engage with them at their level of understanding…to reach their hearts and minds and foster their development. They explore their world at their own pace; we share their discoveries; their world becomes our world; what a privilege it is to learn from them. Unlike us, they do not have preconceived ideas; they are looking at the world as for the first time and are launching upon a great adventure.

Our children will push back the boundaries of knowledge, and it is we who follow them. We notice their openness to the mysteries of the universe, of all that is; there is so much to learn from our children.

Their talents are still to be discovered; do they inherit any of ours? They live their lives with courage and confidence; we support them in their endeavours. Who among us has not marvelled at the young, talented musician who has shown the world that a mature performance of a concerto is possible at the age of ten?

Or that a wonderful painting, fresh and lively, is the work of a small child? Works of genius are by the old and the young alike, and we should remember that.

So, we are grateful for opportunities to encourage our children in all their exploits, be it scaling of the mountains, with all its risks, or the world of music, literature, or art. The whole wide world is to be explored and enjoyed.

We remind ourselves that our children still need our guidance and love as they grow in maturity. If they experience self-doubt, lack of self-worth, or face new challenges in a sometimes-hostile world, they may look to us in their doubting. May we support them in all their many uncertainties as well as in their triumphs.

Penny Johnson

* *Sophia Fahs. American Director of Religious Education.*

FUNERAL PRAYER 1

O God, at this sad time we come to you asking for the special kind of strength and love that only you can give. We shall all have our memories of …………. which we bring here today. No one can take those memories away from us. We hold them in our hearts and cherish them.

We are so thankful for our family and friends, for the loving support we offer to each other; the squeeze of the hand, the hug, the many signs which say, "we care, and will be there for you when you need us most." We may need time to be alone, time to shed tears, time to savour all the precious moments that we shared with…………. Parting is one of the most difficult things we ever have to do, but the affection we shared will never be lost, it remains and sustains us and carries us forward into the future.

Today we express our gratitude for her life amongst us. For the last two years of her life …………..lived at the ………….. Care Home and we are thankful to the staff there, for all the support that they offered to her, and we are grateful that at the end of her life she found herself in such capable hands.

Penny Johnson

FUNERAL PRAYER 2

O God, we come here today, thankful for the many blessings which life has brought us.

Today, as family and friends of ...., we are particularly conscious of our togetherness in bereavement. We sense the loss that each of us feels the very large, unfilled hole left by the death of...............

We recall his kindness and generosity; his love and affection, his/lasting legacy to us through his example of how to live and how to die.

We cannot know the private grief experienced by any one of us, or the pain in our hearts, but we can hold each other tightly, offer each other a hug, remember him often, talk of his influence on us, and ensure that he always remains very firmly within our circle of love and friendship.

Penny Johnson

PRAYER FOR PETS

Dogs and Cats – our family pets. How thankful we are for our dogs and cats, our family pets which need our total care. They each have their personalities and ways of talking to us and making sure that we know exactly what they want. They are members of our family and when they die, they leave large empty spaces in our family circle.

Our dogs look at us with their large sad, doleful eyes, they bring their leads to us with a little woof, hopeful that we shall take them for a walk; they want to play; they make sure that we get exercise.

Our cats are more subtle. They use us as warm, comfortable seats for hours on end; they bring their treasures to us and lay them out in front of us, mice, rabbits, shrews, and look to us to praise them. They treat us with the disdain they think we deserve.

For the loyalty of our dogs, we say, "thank you" and for the contempt of our cats, we say "thank you" also. What a blessing of companionship are our almost human friends.

Penny Johnson

PRAYER FOR A CHURCH OR CHAPEL ANNIVERSARY 1

O God we give thanks for the many blessings which you have bestowed on this congregation over *....... years of its existence. If these walls could speak, they would tell us of the countless triumphs of the human spirit, of courage, of strength, of human capacity to rise to great heights, of ability to carry on when carrying on was almost impossible, of brilliant sermons, and wonderful ministry. These walls would also speak of disappointment, failure, weakness, and loss, of human frailty.

A congregation is made up of all kinds of people, with different qualities, values and abilities, many kinds of aspirations, needs, problems and concerns, but with a common thread, all with a wish to be part of this community, and to give of themselves; to use their gifts wisely and well for the good of all; to develop them in accordance with the highest they know. Everyone takes something from it, and everyone gives something to it.

If these walls could speak, they would tell us of many comings and goings, many births, and deaths; they would speak of differences in the shape and content of sermons, and in varying forms of worship as the years go by.

We are thankful to everyone who has faithfully continued to pass down to us, through the ages, their inspiration. Let us be glad for the fun we enjoy together in this wonderful community here at (name of Church/Chapel). We have so much to celebrate.

Penny Johnson

PRAYER FOR A CHURCH OR CHAPEL ANNIVERSARY 2

O God, as we celebrate our ....anniversary, we are conscious of the many generations of members who have contributed vastly to this place.

For some there has been a life-long commitment. From early years they have shared in its story: Sunday School, Junior Church, Youth Clubs, discussion groups, Women's League, Social activities.

They have been Officers, sat on committees, been active in every aspect of church life, involved with weddings, funerals, church flowers, organ and choir music and cleaned the Chapel building.

Let us not forget anyone who throughout the ages has given their time and expertise to make this Chapel a living memorial to God. Ministers and others who have led worship and provided pastoral care have left their mark.

This community is one body and always will be. From its beginnings there have been a variety of changes to meet the needs and wishes of those who worship here; there have been deaths and new birth, but it is still one body, and as long as this congregation remains it will still be one body of souls who move forward through the ages in one unbroken line.

Can we, by our commitment to it, ensure its continuity? If we value it, "Yes we can."

Penny Johnson

FOR SUMMER

For long summer days and summer nights we are thankful.

Sitting outside on balmy days, picnics, lunch or tea in the garden; watching cricket; the sound of ball on bat; stretching out on a deckchair or garden bed; long walks, hazy-lazy days; the bees busy around the hive; the sound of the mower mowing the lawn; iced water, ice-creams; summer fruits; summer concerts, with bands in the band-stand; sitting by the river fishing; light clothes, flimsy dresses, sandals; river trips, hearing the water lapping; for days at the sea-side, sandcastles, rock pools; a change of pace.

For the summer season we are thankful.

Penny Johnson

FOR HARVEST

O God, for the wonders of this Season, we give thanks. We are grateful to the many people who plough the land, plant the seed, and reap the harvest. For them so much depends on the weather, the quality of the soil, and the faith they have that, in the end, all will be well and the harvest plentiful.

We love the imagery of harvest: we cheerfully sing of the good seed being fed and watered by your almighty hand, and your painting of the wayside flower.

But poetry and fact merge together at harvest-time. Your creative spirit which continues to generate new life needs the efforts of farmers to bring it to fruition, and we pray for their courage in their work to provide the food that we need. They wrestle with all kinds of setbacks from drought and flood to diseases in their crops and in their animals; they sometimes labour under the most appalling conditions.
O God for the wonder of this season, we give thanks.

Penny Johnson

FOR AUTUMN

What a wonderful, colourful season is autumn. There are so many different hues: reds, yellows, orange, browns, a delight which touches all our senses. We see the branches of our fruit trees pulled down by the weight of the fruit, ripe apples, peaches, plums, pears all waiting to be picked and eaten. The homely kitchen smells greet us as we enter the house, jams being made, bottled fruit on the table, apple, and blackberry pies in the oven.

Autumn holds childhood memories: blackberry picking, scrumping apples in orchards, perhaps being caught doing it, carpets of rotting leaves on the ground, the crunchiness of those just fallen from the tree. The sights and smells of autumn pervade the air: John Keats words, "Season of mists and mellow fruitfulness, close bosom friend of the retiring sun" find a space in our hearts. This is autumn at its best, and we are thankful.

Penny Johnson

GOD'S STILL SMALL VOICE

Eternal Spirit bless us with your presence. In the quietness here we sense that you are with us, as you have been with the many generations who have worshipped in this place.

These walls have been made divinely fair by the worship of the ages; we are part of the great community of souls who have generated an abiding holiness and have distilled your love and truth. Here the "past and future blend in one".

In our worship we continue a long and precious tradition of sharing the deep moments of our lives. Sometimes we share more of sorrow than of joy, more anxiety and stress than of peace. We are here with the hope that we shall find answers to problems; and so, seek firstly strength to meet life head on. We pray that you will be with us, supporting us in crises.

We have learned that your still small voice speaks to us in the calm after the storm, but experience teaches us that we can find you right in the middle of the whirlwind, when the storm is raging loudly, and you remain with us as the whirlwind subsides and there is peace at last. You are our rock, and we are thankful.

Penny Johnson

A CHRISTMAS HANUKKA GRACE

In this season of festivity when families and friends come together to share meals and conversation, we are thankful for good food and good company.

O God bless us all.

Peter Hewis

MORE GRACES

May our prayer be a simple one -

That all people everywhere will have food to eat,
water to drink and friends to meet.

May the spirit of the eternal be at this table
and in the hearts of all we know and love.

May we value those who sit at the table with us,
be grateful for our common interests
and for the fraternity that we share.

To this table we welcome many people,
May we enjoy our time together in this friendly company and may
the universal spirit be with us all.

May we give mutual help to each other on this day and always,
May we have the vision of Moses, the wisdom of Solomon, the patience of Job, and follow the example of Jesus.

Peter Hewis

WITHIN THE COMMON, THE DIVINE

Source of all life,
We pray that we might be able to see, within the common, the divine. May we all take a fresh look at life and be invigorated by the simple things.

Some of us think we have grown old, for us may we realise the wondrous enchantment of a child looking at a jar of tadpoles, or a child looking at a battered but beloved doll or teddy bear. Then may we realise that although our bodies are old our hearts are eternally young.

Some amongst us are young; we have a zest for living and are often impatient for action. May we look at an elderly couple choosing a present for a grandchild or tending the garden. Then may we realise that they too were once young in body and had eager zest but now have the patience to live life at a leisurely pace and tend a garden.

Whatever our age may we see, "Within the common, the divine." May we see it every day, in a bowl of flowers, in animals, in the letters pushed through our door, in children and most of all, in the people whom we love.

If at times our love and trust are betrayed let us never despair, but may we keep our faith in times of stress and continue to search for the divine. May we always remember that money, intellect, and power cannot buy divinity for divinity is freely to be found in every walk of life and especially in the common, ordinary, every-day things of life.

Peter Hewis

Originally written for the mixed ages at Broadway Avenue Church in Bradford and based on Hosmer's hymn, "We pray no more, made lowly wise, for miracle and sign; anoint our eyes to see, within the common, the divine."

FOR MINISTERS IN A FREE FAITH

Eternal Spirit,

We bring thankful hearts for the privilege that is ours to be Ministers within a free religious faith,
To be interpreters of life and eternity,
To be prophets and teachers, comforters, and inspirers,
To join with families in celebrating birth, commitment, and times of sorrow.

We are thankful for the faith that people place in us to be conscientious, honest, and truthful.

May we be conscious of the noble Ministers of old, people like Martineau, Emerson, Parker, and Channing, may we be conscious of the many humble souls within our Ministry who never became famous yet bore the heat and burden of the day, all those women and men that humbly served their people and their community.

May we follow in their fine and noble tradition.

Peter Hewis

FOR CHESTER CATHEDERAL
AS WE LIT A CHALICE

Eternal Spirit,
As we sense the atmosphere of this ancient cathedral and feel the warmth of its sandstone walls and its people, made reverent by the worship of ages, may we too feel a sense of warmth, reverence, and awe.

May the walls surrounding this city of Chester wrap around us to remind us of the need for communities of faith. We pray that something from our worship will reach out to the people of this city, to those descended from the earliest citizens, to those of Roman descent and to all those that have arrived in more recent times.

As we see the flame of our own chalice, we pray that the light of a single candle will shine in our own lives and enable us to carry that same light into our churches, chapels, and many gatherings throughout our nations. May that same light be taken and carried to our friends across the world.

We call to mind our own community of faith, the places where our people have suffered or are suffering persecution and great difficulties, may the gentle chalice light shine out to give them warmth, light, and hope.

May our chalice flame be like a prayer for all people, like a parable speaking of eternal things and may the flame be a symbol of love and hope, of light and warmth.

Peter Hewis

Written for the Unitarian General Assembly service in Chester Cathedral when we were made so welcome by Canon Trevor Dennis. A year later Unitarians were banned by the Bishop from worshipping there!

FOR COVENTRY, 350 YEARS OF WORSHIP & 75 YEARS IN THEIR PRESENT CHURCH

Eternal Spirit,

In this Meeting House may we be conscious of all those people in the past who created the tradition of religious freedom, often meeting and worshipping together in secret but always upholding the torch of religious freedom.

We remember those courageous people from three hundred and fifty years ago who had the courage to stand up for their beliefs. We give thanks for the Meeting House that they built in Smithford Street so long ago.

We give thanks too for those who had the vision some seventy-five years ago to move from the city centre to this site.

We bring grateful hearts for all the ministers that have served this church and especially this day for Richard Lee who led his people to this spot and who firmly believed in education for all. We pray for all the children and staff of the school named after him.

In our prayers let us think of all Coventrians who live in this fine city and of those who suffered bereavement in World War II.

We pray for those who meet in this place and keep it alive so that it can serve the wider community.

May we all pray for three simple things:

That people everywhere will have food to eat and water to drink - and that people everywhere will have the freedom to worship in their own way without the need of harming others.

Peter Hewis

*Although this was for a special event it can easily
be adapted for any town or city*

THE GATHERING

We gather in this Meeting House as others have gathered for almost three hundred years. As we gather may we be mindful of the contributions made by so many people in order that we might gather and worship today.

The red bricks remind us of human endeavour, the mortar reminds us of our human bonds. The golden glow of the oak panelling tells us of warmth, the flowers before us remind us of a world of beauty and nature, the memorials speak of benefactors named and unnamed; our pulpit tells us of ideals and ideas.

As we gather within these walls, may we be conscious of all those that have cared for, and still care for this our place of worship.

O Eternal, may we find the best of human life in this our Meeting House, may we recognize that of God in every human being and may we leave this Meeting House for those that will follow in our footsteps.

Peter Hewis

*Originally written for the anniversary of the
Great Meeting Chapel, Hinckley.*

WEALTH IN MANY VAULTS

Many years ago, a man of Lithuanian origin who had won two million pounds on the football pools refused to let Littlewoods buy him a new suit for the glittery presentation. One of his dreams was to buy a dog and call the dog "Rebel." I realised that all the money would not change the man's outlook on life for he enjoys simple pleasures, his wealth is in many vaults.

Our wealth is contained in many vaults.
in the vaults of childhood, of neighbours and school friends and in the games that we played long ago.

in the vaults of home, in the sharing of life with brothers, sisters, cousins, aunts and uncles, parents and grandparents.

in the vaults of places and communities, our town, our church, or chapel, in an organization, Scouts, Guides, youth clubs and social groups.

Our wealth is contained in the vaults of relationships; marriage, children, grandchildren, in the close friendships of adult life, in those deep relationships that cannot even be described in words.

Our wealth is in vaults of love that we give or receive; in the love that is given for no other motive than that of giving.

Our wealth is in the vaults of music, songs, words, and thoughts. Our wealth is here in this Meeting House, with each one of us and amongst our people today.

For all this great wealth in many vaults may we be thankful.

Peter Hewis

NOW WRITE YOUR PRAYER OR MEDITATION

You might start by thinking about some of the things below.

What am I grateful for and what is most precious to me?

What people mean the most to me and have influenced my life?

Who have I hurt in my lifetime and from whom I need forgiveness?

Sunrise and sunset, the sea, a lake, precious water.

The treasures of my garden.

Birds of many kinds.

What music has affected me?

A favourite building, its walls, windows, furnishings, the people inside.

ACKNOWLEDGEMENTS

We would like to offer our special thanks to Natasha Stanley for all her help in turning our ideas into reality.

We would also like to give special thanks to the Manchester District Association of Unitarian & Free Christian Churches for their financial sponsorship.

NOTES

Printed in Great Britain
by Amazon

74732212R00058